Poets From Norfolk & Suffolk

Edited By Machaela Gavaghan

First published in Great Britain in 2019 by:

Young Writers
Remus House
Coltsfoot Drive
Peterborough
PE2 9BF
Telephone: 01733 890066
Website: www.youngwriters.co.uk

Foreword

Dear Reader,

Are you ready to explore the wonderful delights of poetry?

Young Writers' *Poetry Patrol* gang set out to encourage and ignite the imaginations of 5-7 year-olds as they took their first steps into the magical world of poetry. With **Riddling Rabbit**, **Acrostic Croc** and **Sensory Skunk** on hand to help, children were invited to write an acrostic, sense poem or riddle on any theme, from people to places, animals to objects, food to seasons. *Poetry Patrol* is also a great way to introduce children to the use of poetic expression, including onomatopoeia and similes, repetition and metaphors, acting as stepping stones for their future poetic journey.

All of us here at Young Writers believe in the importance of inspiring young children to produce creative writing, including poetry, and we feel that seeing their own poem in print will keep that creative spirit burning brightly and proudly.

We hope you enjoy reading this wonderful collection as much as we enjoyed reading all the entries.

Contents

Earthsea School, Honingham

Eternity Sharpe (7)	59
Jay Peacher (8)	60

Freethorpe Community Primary School, Freethorpe

Darcy Howlett (6)	61
Alice Key (7)	62
Hugo Ball (6)	64
Poppy Sykes (6)	65
Kiara Clark (6)	66
Sarah Anne Vos (6)	67

Hockering CE (VC) Primary School, Hockering

Emily Brend (6)	68
Leo Surrel-Parfitt (7)	69
Gracie Reading (6)	70
Swaylee Olley-Kelf (7)	71
Mia Spinks (5)	72
Savanna Olley-Kelf (6)	73

Kyson Primary School, Woodbridge

Layla Rogers (6)	74
Lylia Grace Bailey (6)	75
Oliver Dale (6)	76
Amani Okello (6)	77
Finn Milbourn (5)	78
Delilah Ann Morris (6)	79
Freya Grace Chowdhury (5)	80
Georgia O'Shaughnessy (5)	81
Tobias Wilson (6)	82
Scarlett Sargent (6)	83
Lewis Brumby (5)	84
Lucy Walker (5)	85
Henry Pope (6)	86
Matilda Longe (6)	87
Jack Dodwell (6)	88
Dylan Garnham (6)	89
Maisie Adams (6)	90

Arthur Dickins (6)	91
Isaac Chandler (6)	92
Logan Brinley Carrington (5)	93
Myles Hutchinson (5)	94
Connor Giles (5)	95
Yoan Zhivkov (5) & Henry David Barnard	96
George Mitson (6)	97
Tilly Hinton (6)	98
Albie Hamnett (6)	99

Middleton Primary School, Middleton

Orlando Montgomery Dino Burns-Tucker (5)	100
Dani Gallagher (7)	101
Chloe Long (6)	102
Anna Griffiths (6)	103
Beau Cecil James Burn-Tucker (5)	104
Percy Reynolds (6)	105

Norwich Primary Academy, Norwich

Toby Luptak (6)	106
Beate Odrija Avina (7)	107
Harry David Allen (6)	108
Tudor Ianis Negraru (6)	109
Phoebe Grady (6)	110
Leia Batson (7)	111
Kyra Young (7)	112
Cyril Chigozie Akomah (6)	113
Rio Walker (6)	114
Kayden Rogers (6)	115
Zofia Misztal (6)	116
Izzy Burrows (7)	117
Csenge Toth (6)	118
Riley Ayre (6)	119
Lily-Louise Callaway (6)	120
Josie-Rose Christine Leader (7)	121
Cameron Marshall (7)	122

Suffield Park Infant School, Cromer

Jennyfer May Rippingale (6)	123
Amelie Medler (6)	124
Jessica Folwer (6)	125
Mollie Taylor (7)	126
Raj Dorras (6)	127
Willow Elizabeth Davis (7)	128
Riley Stokes (6)	129
Noah Crane (6)	130
Luke Records (6)	131
Sidney Jonas (7)	132
Isabella Waplington (6)	133
Rokas Kriksciunas (6)	134
Sebastian Edward-Ipperciel (7)	135
Bella Vanzino (7)	136
Olga Fox (6)	137
Ethan McVeigh (7)	138
Chloe Findlay (6)	139
Migle Mickeviciute (7)	140
Jacob Grant (7)	141
Andre Bandarra (6)	142
Darcie Goodwin (7)	143
Patryk Imienionek (6)	144
Hayley Jena Chatten (7)	145
Emelia McVeigh (7)	146
William Smith (7)	147
Elicia Garcia (6)	148
Chelsea Gao (6)	149
Evie Plummer (6)	150
Cody Pegg (6)	151

The Poems

Our Own Book

I have cheeks as red as a poppy.
I have a cape as red as fire.
I have a hat attached to my cape.
I have a mum.
In my book, there is a woodcutter.
In my book, there is a wolf.
I have a garden.
I have lots of flowers.
Who am I?

Answer: Little Red Riding Hood.

Lilliarna McInally (6)
Astley Primary School, Briston

Abracadabra!

He has cracked glasses.
He likes making spells.
He has scruffy, brown hair.
He has a magic wand.
He has a bruise on his head.
He has circled glasses.
He lost his mum and dad.
He is a big boy.
Who is he?

Answer: Harry Potter.

Sophie Clark (7)
Astley Primary School, Briston

Monster Switch

I am green and really shiny.
I can turn into a monster.
I can change like a caterpillar.
I have a green and black watch.
I have a green screen on my watch.
Who am I?

Answer: Ben 10.

Ethan O'Donoughoe (7)
Astley Primary School, Briston

Time For Magic

I am a girl
I have a brown wand
I have brown hair
I am out of Harry Potter
I have a time twister necklace
and it takes me back in time
Who am I?

Answer: Hermoine Granger.

Maisy James (6)
Astley Primary School, Briston

Magic Wands

I have a magic wand
I have black glasses
I have a scar on my forehead
I love doing magic
My glasses are as black as midnight
I love Dobby
Who am I?

Answer: Harry Potter.

Tallulah Basham (7)
Astley Primary School, Briston

Christmastime

I have a dad that loves Christmas.
I have a strange pet
called the Christmasaurus.
I have a big quiff in my hair
and I love dinosaurs.
Who am I?

Answer: William Trundle.

Max Williams (7)
Astley Primary School, Briston

The Chocolate Factory

I am very cunning.
I've got a shiny, black top hat.
I've got a cloak as pink as the rainbow.
I own an amazing chocolate factory.
Who am I?

Answer: Willy Wonka.

Ned Tosney (6)
Astley Primary School, Briston

A Special Thing

I have black, round glasses
I have a long, strong robe
I have a magic wand
I have a broomstick
that is as fast as a cheetah
Who am I?

Answer: Harry Potter.

Tilly Martha Elderton (7)
Astley Primary School, Briston

Who Am I?

I have a stick as long as a tree branch
and it has a beam.
I can be any colour.
I am round.
I am a good fighter.
Who am I?

Answer: Beam Kirby.

Tommy Brady (7)
Astley Primary School, Briston

A Cold Day

I am as big as an elephant.
I am big, brown and furry.
I have lots of soldier friends.
Two girls love me.
Who am I?

Answer: *The Ice Monster.*

Sophia Louise Hopper (7)
Astley Primary School, Briston

Batman's Friend

I live in an orphanage
I have glasses
I have a red jumper
I have brown hair
My favourite superhero is Batman
Who am I?

Answer: Robin.

Harry Christopher Wright (6)
Astley Primary School, Briston

A Special Visitor

I have a tail
I have blue scales
I am a dinosaur
I am as fast as a car
I am as white as snow
What am I?

Answer: The Christmasaurus.

Oliver Bailey-Platten (6)
Astley Primary School, Briston

The Witch

I have three sisters.
We all begin with a 'W'.
I have a black cat.
I have a pointy hat.
Who am I?

Answer: Winnie the Witch.

Lily May Goldsmith-Browne (7)

Astley Primary School, Briston

Tudors

I was a Tudor king.
Mostly, I eat meat.
My name begins with 'H'.
I was the second Tudor king.
Who am I?

Answer: Henry VIII.

Thomas Quinlan (6)
Astley Primary School, Briston

What Am I?

I have snowflake patterns down my back
I have a long tail with spikes on it
I live in Antarctica
What am I?

Answer: The Christmasaurus.

Otillie Ngaio Danger Deans (7)

Astley Primary School, Briston

Tall Poetry

I am massive.
I am twenty-five metres tall.
All I get to eat is snozzcumbers.
I am as big as a sofa.
Who am I?

Answer: The BFG.

Bertie Bowes (6)
Astley Primary School, Briston

Mysterious Mysteries

I have detective glasses.
I ponder all the time.
I have a crime HQ.
I have a thinking chair.
Who am I?

Answer: Saxby Smart.

Noah Henry Forsyth (7)
Astley Primary School, Briston

A Strong Man

His muscles are strong
He has a red bandana
His skin is green
He has big pads
Who is he?

Answer: Raphael the Ninja Turtle.

Seb Rutland (6)
Astley Primary School, Briston

Who Am I?

I bully people
I have an annoying brother
I play tricks on everyone
I like watching TV
Who am I?

Answer: Horrid Henry.

Demi Ashton Lee (7)

Astley Primary School, Briston

Who Am I?

I have black, fluffy hair
I have stripy clothes
I am stinky
I have a little brother
Who am I?

Answer: Horrid Henry.

George Edward Van Coller (7)
Astley Primary School, Briston

Who Am I?

I am an elf.
I have magic at night.
I do something magical
but you have to be asleep.
Who am I?

Answer: Elfy.

Rory James Hunt (6)
Astley Primary School, Briston

Who Is He?

He has a cape.
He wears underpants like a superhero.
He saves the world.
Who is he?

Answer: Captain Underpants.

Leo-Jay Kettell (6)
Astley Primary School, Briston

A Stripy Man

I wear stripy clothes.
I like to hide.
I wear red and white.
Who am I?

Answer: Where's Wally?

Billy Copeman (6)
Astley Primary School, Briston

Who Am I?

I am really greedy.
I am pink and fat.
I eat any food.
Who am I?

Answer: Mr Greedy.

Austin Hilling (6)
Astley Primary School, Briston

Summer

In summer, we go to camp
I really hope my brother won't stamp
On my bed in the tent
I really hope he meant
To stand on my sister's instead
I like to eat
The barbecue meat
Cooked by my dad
It's not too bad
Ice cream for a sweet
I like to eat
Hot chocolate for bed
And a cuddle with Ted.

Casey Christian (6)
Browick Road Primary School, Wymondham

I'm Going To Eat You

D eep, dark voice

I nside a dark cave

N ice to his dinosaur friends but not to others

O h, I see a dinosaur!

"S orry, I have to eat you!"

A rgh! I'm being chased by a dinosaur!

U h-oh, he's seen me...

R *oar!*

Emily Bassett (7)
Browick Road Primary School, Wymondham

Chocolate

C hocolate is yummy
H ow do you eat it?
O h, why don't you like chocolate?
C hocolate is the best!
O h, it's my favourite treat
L ove it, don't you?
A lovely treat to eat
T asty and yummy
E at it all up!

Finn Garrihy (6)

Browick Road Primary School, Wymondham

Autumn

Autumn tastes like pumpkins
jumping down my throat.
Autumn looks like
harvest festival celebrations.
Autumn sounds like gunpowder crackling.
Autumn smells like old and dry leaves
and smoke from dusty cars.
Autumn feels like old, dusty
and misty pathways.

Hartley Morgan-Rossiter (7)
Browick Road Primary School, Wymondham

Who Am I?

I fly in the sky.
I blow fire extremely bright.
I live in a cave.
I have big wings to fly in the sky.
I can roar loudly.
I can walk on the land.
Who am I?

Answer: Zog the dragon.

Aaliyah James (6)
Browick Road Primary School, Wymondham

Summer Is...

Summer looks like the light from the sun
Summer sounds like people on the beach
Summer smells like ice cream
Summer feels like burning backs
Summer tastes like picnics
Summer is a winner!

Lois Mack (6)
Browick Road Primary School, Wymondham

Fun Rugby

R unning around on the pitch
U nder the posts, scoring lots of tries
G reat fun
B all has to be passed backwards
Y ummy hot dogs after the lesson is done.

Toby Hewson (7)
Browick Road Primary School, Wymondham

Ho, Ho, Ho

S anta comes down the chimney
A roast is cooking
N ow families are coming together
T oys are being made
A man gets on his sleigh with his reindeer.

Amelia Buckenham (6)
Browick Road Primary School, Wymondham

What Am I?

I am fluffy and soft
I am small and funny
I am white and brown
I dig from my home
What am I?

Answer: A rabbit.

Amelia Miller (7)
Browick Road Primary School, Wymondham

Fabulous Flowers

F abulous flowers swaying in the trees

L ovely lilies floating on the blue see-through pond

O range flowers dancing slowly through the air

W iggly worms wiggling through the winter wind

E merald flowers swaying through the elegant trees

R uby-red roses ready to be picked

S uper speedy flowers growing quickly.

Pippa Lane (7)
Bures CE (VC) Primary School, Bures

A Lovely Flower Garden

A lovely waterlily floating in the water
A lovely rose growing from the ground
A daffodil shining in the sun
A daisy glowing in the sun
The flowers are all growing
A lion steps into the wave of grass
A parrot flies into the shiny sky
A penguin skates on the ice
A skunk rides down a wavy river.

Ellouise Morley (6)
Bures CE (VC) Primary School, Bures

A Garden

G roovy grass growing fast

A mazing animals running around the hutch quickly

R ed roses growing calmly

D omed dens being built quickly

E merald trees sway calmly

N eat and tidy bunches of flowers are picked.

Huckleberry Robinson (6)
Bures CE (VC) Primary School, Bures

A Lovely Flower Garden

G olden grass growing quickly

A mazing ants eating leaves

R uby-red roses dancing

D elightful daisies dancing in the wind

E xcited, elegant emeralds swaying

N asty, naughty nettles fighting.

Lyla-Rose Brasier (7)

Bures CE (VC) Primary School, Bures

The Scented Garden

F abulous flowers swaying fast
L uscious little lupins
O rchids glide slowly
W onderful waterlilies
E legant flowers grow
R uby-red roses
S unflowers, bright and yellow.

Hope Baldwin (7)

Bures CE (VC) Primary School, Bures

Little Trees

F lowers swaying in the wind
L ovely grass swaying
O live trees swaying in the wind
W onderful breeze
E legantly blowing
R oses swaying in the wind
S oft roses.

Evie Rose Nash (6)

Bures CE (VC) Primary School, Bures

Flowers

F lowers growing

L ovely roses

O range flowers dance

E legantly in the wind

E xcellent flowers

R ed tulips smell lovely

S tunning and super speedy.

George Cousins (6)
Bures CE (VC) Primary School, Bures

The Sweet-Scented Garden

I can smell the lovely smell of a red flower.
I can see the prickles of a stem.
I can feel the smooth petals waving their
lovely leaves slowly in the air.
I can hear the birds singing loudly.

Freya Byford (6)

Bures CE (VC) Primary School, Bures

A Lovely, Lovely Garden

F lowing flowers
L ovely lilies float calmly
O range marigolds and
W aterlilies
E merald leaves
R uby-red roses and
S illy bluebells.

Evie Povall (6)
Bures CE (VC) Primary School, Bures

An Exotic Animal

I have been found in Morocco.
I have four legs.
I am scared of Tom Cats.
I'm shy.
I am covered in spotty fur.
What am I?

Answer: I am a spotted genet.

Eleanor Frewin (7)
Bures CE (VC) Primary School, Bures

Flowers In The Garden

F abulous flowers

L ovely clouds

O range flowers blowing in the wind

W aterlilies in the wind

E legant poppies

R uby-red petals.

Florence Coe (6)

Bures CE (VC) Primary School, Bures

The Sweet-Scented Flower

I can see a white, milky flower
It is like a wedding flower
The mint smells of toothpaste
Fresh and spiky, like a pine tree
I can feel bumpy seeds.

Eliza Campbell (7)
Bures CE (VC) Primary School, Bures

A Fluffy And Puffy Animal

It bites
It has beautiful eyes
It is fluffy and short
It is full of hair and has sheep legs
What is it?

Answer: A Chow Chow.

Noah Joseph (6)
Bures CE (VC) Primary School, Bures

The Scented Garden

A sweet-smelling, white-looking flower
It reminds me of the sea
And I can hear the noises, *swoosh, swoosh!*

William Jenkins (7)
Bures CE (VC) Primary School, Bures

My African Animal

I live in the zoo.
I have four legs.
I eat grass.
What am I?

Answer: A giraffe.

Lilly Roberts (6)
Bures CE (VC) Primary School, Bures

A Winter Walk

Crunching, wet grass under our feet
And old, slippery puddles
The thin ice is cracking
In the freezing cold
Icy breaths in the white clouds
Red noses in the chilly air
The puddles are hard and frozen.

Charlotte H (7)

Capel St Mary CE (VC) Primary School, Capel St Mary

A Winter Walk

Slippery ice
Cold, slippery ice
Big, slippery ice
Frosty grass
It's all on our noses
The ice is cracking
Red noses in the cold, chilly air
The ice is slippery
With icy, bare trees.

Lucy W (7)

Capel St Mary CE (VC) Primary School, Capel St Mary

Winter

W et snow falling down
 I ce falling down
N ice and thick ice
T eeth shivering
E ating hot chocolate
R unning about in the snow leaving
   footprints.

Evie Rout (7)

Capel St Mary CE (VC) Primary School, Capel St
Mary

Winter

W inter is cold

I cy, spiky paths

N othing is dry

T rees are icy and cold

E verything is wet

R ivers are frozen.

Charlie Jack Cunningham (6)

Capel St Mary CE (VC) Primary School, Capel St Mary

A Winter Walk

The frosty grass is wet on our hands
And hard enough to stand on
Cold on my fingers, bare trees
The roses are red
The ice is white and wet.

Fraser Payne (6)

Capel St Mary CE (VC) Primary School, Capel St Mary

A Winter Walk

The cold, frosty grass is a little cold
With numb fingers, the trees are frosty
The evenings are cold and frosty
The fluffy snow is cold.

Matilda Seager (6)
Capel St Mary CE (VC) Primary School, Capel St Mary

A Winter Walk

F rozen gardens

R ain and water

O n the grass

S now on the grass

T asty marshmallows.

Henry H (6)
Capel St Mary CE (VC) Primary School, Capel St Mary

Snow

S nowflakes falling from the sky

N ice snowballs

O n the grass

W hite ice is cold.

Mason Mitchell (6)

Capel St Mary CE (VC) Primary School, Capel St Mary

Snow

S now is pouring down
N ot that much
O n my jumper
W hite snow.

Lewis Goddard (7)

Capel St Mary CE (VC) Primary School, Capel St Mary

A Winter Walk

An icy storm
The puddles are frozen
It is cold
The frosty grass has wet our hands.

Bobby Mayhew (7)
Capel St Mary CE (VC) Primary School, Capel St
Mary

A Kitten

K now your pet
I t is nice
T abby kittens are pretty
T iny kittens are beautiful
E nergetic kittens are fluffy
N ice and cuddly.

Eternity Sharpe (7)
Earthsea School, Honingham

Cars

C ars on the road
A n F1 car
R emember to put on the brakes
S uper fast.

Jay Peacher (8)
Earthsea School, Honingham

Gymnastics

G ymnastics is my favourite thing to do
Y ou can tumble, you can swing like a
   monkey in the zoo
M ummy watches me from afar
N ever falling off the parallel bar
A big cartwheel through the air
S plits on the floor like I just don't care
T rampolining, doing spins
I n the gym, everyone wins
C olourful leotard, sparkles and shine
S o much fun, I do it all the time.

Darcy Howlett (6)
Freethorpe Community Primary School, Freethorpe

I Live On A Farm

I live on a farm
It's really good fun
There are lots of places
To play and to run

There's tractors and mud
There's cows and there's straw
With so much to do
It's never a bore

In winter sometimes
There are calves to look after
They chew on our coats
And we have lots of laughter

Summer is harvest
And it's a real treat
To ride in the combine
On the spare seat

When I grow up
Let's wait and see
But maybe a farmer
Is what I will be?

Alice Key (7)

Freethorpe Community Primary School, Freethorpe

Sharks

S cary sharks chasing seals
H unting for a tasty meal
A ngry sharks in the reef
R azor-sharp triangle teeth
K iller sharks, killer sharks

B ig and fierce in the sea
I really hope they don't catch me!
T asty meals for a hungry shark
E ating under the sea, so dark.

Hugo Ball (6)
Freethorpe Community Primary School, Freethorpe

The Pets

I have got a dog
Who thinks he is a frog
He has got a puppy
Who loves chasing guppies
When they go and swim together
The dog is very clever
And never, ever, ever
Swims in the cold, rainy weather
Once, the dog met a cat
Who thought he was a rat
He had a kitten
Who loved sitting on mittens.

Poppy Sykes (6)
Freethorpe Community Primary School, Freethorpe

Flowers Are Beautiful

F lowers blow in the wind

L ovely and colourful

O ne and more grow when you plant them

W e love flowers and plants

E very flower is beautiful

R eal flowers need water

S unshine is bright in the sky.

Kiara Clark (6)

Freethorpe Community Primary School, Freethorpe

Unicorn Sparkles

U p in the sky so blue
N ice to me and you
I n a nice beautiful land
C alm and beautiful
O nly the best for you
R ed and green sparkles too
N o one is as pretty as you.

Sarah Anne Vos (6)

Freethorpe Community Primary School, Freethorpe

What Am I?

I am a fierce dinosaur.
I am a meat eater.
I have over sixty teeth.
I eat other dinosaurs.
I have a long tail.
I am very strong.
I have long claws.
My name means tyrant lizard.
What am I?

Answer: A T-rex.

Emily Brend (6)
Hockering CE (VC) Primary School, Hockering

What Am I?

I am a meat eater.
I lived a long time ago.
I have sharp teeth.
I have a long tail.
I have short arms.
I am a fierce dinosaur.
What am I?

Answer: A T-rex.

Leo Surrel-Parfitt (7)
Hockering CE (VC) Primary School, Hockering

What Am I?

I have spikes on my hands
I eat leaves
I have a sharp tail
I lived a long time ago
What am I?

Answer: An iguanodon.

Gracie Reading (6)
Hockering CE (VC) Primary School, Hockering

What Am I?

I am a herbivore
I have spikes on my back
I have a small head
I eat plants
What am I?

Answer: An ankylosaurus.

Swaylee Olley-Kelf (7)
Hockering CE (VC) Primary School, Hockering

What Am I?

I am a dinosaur
I eat leaves
I have a long neck
I have four legs
What am I?

Answer: A brachiosaurus.

Mia Spinks (5)
Hockering CE (VC) Primary School, Hockering

What Am I?

I lived a long time ago
I eat leaves
I have a long neck
What am I?

Answer: An diplodocus.

Savanna Olley-Kelf (6)

Hockering CE (VC) Primary School, Hockering

Autumn

Autumn looks like falling leaves.
Autumn sounds like the wind
howling around the trees.
Autumn smells like finished sparklers
and fireworks.
Autumn feels like watery eyes
on a windy day.
Autumn tastes like delicious hot dogs
on Bonfire Night.
Autumn is fun.

Layla Rogers (6)
Kyson Primary School, Woodbridge

Spring

Spring looks like the bright blue sky.
Spring sounds like people
busy in their gardens.
Spring smells like chocolate Easter eggs.
Spring feels like my Easter basket
in my hand.
Spring tastes like tasty fish and salty chips.
Spring is happy.

Lylia Grace Bailey (6)

Kyson Primary School, Woodbridge

Spring

Spring looks like blossom
falling from the trees.
Spring sounds like nature waking up.
Spring smells like chocolate Easter eggs.
Spring feels like my Easter basket
in my hand.
Spring tastes like tasty fish and salty chips.
Spring is lovely.

Oliver Dale (6)

Kyson Primary School, Woodbridge

Summer

Summer looks like children
eating cold ice cream.
Summer sounds like pigeons flapping.
Summer smells like your dad
mowing the grass.
Summer feels like the warm sand.
Summer tastes like cold
slippery ice cream.
Summer is adventurous.

Amani Okello (6)
Kyson Primary School, Woodbridge

Autumn

Autumn looks like colourful
sparkly fireworks.
Autumn sounds like crackling fires.
Autumn smells like smoky fires
on Bonfire Night.
Autumn feels like cosy boots on my feet.
Autumn tastes like chips with ketchup.
Autumn is snuggly.

Finn Milbourn (5)

Kyson Primary School, Woodbridge

Spring

Spring looks like colourful, bright blossom.
Spring sounds like yellow chirping chicks.
Spring smells like beautiful, fresh flowers.
Spring feels like the sun is getting closer.
Spring tastes like delicious Easter eggs.
Spring is magical!

Delilah Ann Morris (6)
Kyson Primary School, Woodbridge

Spring

Spring looks like colourful, bright blossom.
Spring sounds like yellow chirping chicks.
Spring smells like beautiful, fresh flowers.
Spring feels like the sun is getting closer.
Spring tastes like a lamb roast dinner.
Spring is magical.

Freya Grace Chowdhury (5)
Kyson Primary School, Woodbridge

Autumn

Autumn looks like falling leaves.
Autumn sounds like the whistling wind.
Autumn smells like finished sparklers
and fireworks.
Autumn feels like cosy boots on my feet.
Autumn tastes like nice chips with ketchup.
Autumn is snuggly.

Georgia O'Shaughnessy (5)
Kyson Primary School, Woodbridge

Summer

Summer looks like the hot, shining sun.
Summer sounds like the birds
tweeting happily.
Summer smells like perfumed flowers.
Summer feels like hot sand on your feet.
Summer tastes like yummy, cold ice cream.
Summer is fantastic.

Tobias Wilson (6)
Kyson Primary School, Woodbridge

Spring

Spring looks like buzzing bees
collecting nectar.
Spring sounds like nature waking up.
Spring smells like chocolate Easter eggs.
Spring feels like soft, smooth leaves.
Spring tastes like tasty fish and chips.
Spring is lovely.

Scarlett Sargent (6)

Kyson Primary School, Woodbridge

Summer

Summer looks like brightly-coloured clothes.
Summer sounds like the music
from an ice cream van.
Summer smells like Dad mowing the grass.
Summer feels like warm sand.
Summer tastes like lip-licking barbecues.
Summer is crazy.

Lewis Brumby (5)
Kyson Primary School, Woodbridge

Winter

Winter looks like white, sparkling snow.
Winter sounds like Santa's bell
ringing loudly.
Winter smells like burning log fires.
Winter feels like frost on your face.
Winter tastes like a tasty mince pie.
Winter is magical.

Lucy Walker (5)

Kyson Primary School, Woodbridge

Summer

Summer looks like the hot, shining sun.
Summer sounds like children
playing outside.
Summer smells like sizzling barbecues.
Summer feels like hot sand on your feet.
Summer tastes like delicious barbecue food.
Summer is fun.

Henry Pope (6)
Kyson Primary School, Woodbridge

Autumn

Autumn looks like falling leaves.
Autumn sounds like the whistling wind.
Autumn smells like sweet
gooey, toffee apples.
Autumn feels like the wild wind on my face.
Autumn tastes like nice chips with ketchup.
Autumn is fun.

Matilda Longe (6)
Kyson Primary School, Woodbridge

Winter

Winter looks like frosty, cold weather.
Winter sounds like Santa's bells
ringing loudly.
Winter smells like log fires.
Winter feels like freezing cold hands.
Winter tastes like a chocolate log.
Winter is exciting.

Jack Dodwell (6)
Kyson Primary School, Woodbridge

Summer

Summer looks like brightly-coloured clothes.
Summer sounds like birds tweeting happily.
Summer smells like daisies in my garden
Summer feels like a hat on my head
Summer tastes like mouth-watering
barbecues
Summer is wild.

Dylan Garnham (6)
Kyson Primary School, Woodbridge

Autumn

Autumn looks like leaves falling
from the trees.
Autumn sounds like crunching leaves.
Autumn smells like bonfire smoke.
Autumn feels wet and cold.
Autumn tastes like pumpkin pie
on Halloween.
Autumn is exciting!

Maisie Adams (6)
Kyson Primary School, Woodbridge

Summer

Summer looks like the sunny seaside.
Summer sounds like children
playing outside.
Summer smells like sizzling barbecues.
Summer feels like hot sand on your feet.
Summer tastes like cold ice cream.
Summer is exciting.

Arthur Dickins (6)

Kyson Primary School, Woodbridge

Spring

Spring looks like the bright blue sky.
Spring sounds like nature waking up.
Spring smells like chocolate Easter eggs.
Spring feels like soft, smooth leaves.
Spring tastes like tasty fish and salty chips.
Spring is lovely.

Isaac Chandler (6)

Kyson Primary School, Woodbridge

Summer

Summer looks like people splashing in the
paddling pool.
Summer sounds like birds tweeting.
Summer smells like daisies on hilltops.
Summer feels like a hat on my head.
Summer tastes like cold ice cream.
Summer is wild.

Logan Brinley Carrington (5)

Kyson Primary School, Woodbridge

Winter

Winter looks like cold, frosty weather.
Winter sounds like Santa's bells ringing.
Winter smells like burning log fires.
Winter feels like frost on your face.
Winter tastes like a tasty mince pie.
Winter is magical.

Myles Hutchinson (5)
Kyson Primary School, Woodbridge

Spring

Spring looks like beautiful, bright blossom.
Spring sounds like the hum of lawnmowers.
Spring smells like freshly-cut grass.
Spring feels like a warm breeze.
Spring tastes like delicious Easter eggs.
Spring is magical.

Connor Giles (5)

Kyson Primary School, Woodbridge

Winter

Winter looks like bare, brown trees.
Winter sounds like crunchy snow.
Winter smells like fresh air.
Winter feels like frosty, cold snow.
Winter tastes like delicious, yummy turkey.
Winter is joyful.

Yoan Zhivkov (5) & Henry David Barnard
Kyson Primary School, Woodbridge

Summer

Summer looks like the sunny seaside.
Summer sounds like the birds
tweeting happily.
Summer sounds like barbecues sizzling.
Summer feels like the hot sun on your face.
Summer is fun.

George Mitson (6)
Kyson Primary School, Woodbridge

Spring

Spring looks like colourful, beautiful
blossom.
Spring sounds like chirping.
Spring smells like freshly-cut grass.
Spring feels like a warm breeze.
Spring is fantastic.

Tilly Hinton (6)
Kyson Primary School, Woodbridge

Spring

Spring smells like freshly-cut grass
Spring feels like a warm breeze
Spring is magical!

Albie Hamnett (6)

Kyson Primary School, Woodbridge

A Penguin

P addling in the freezing sea

E ating yummy fish from the ocean

N o one can live here, only visit

G roup of emperor penguins huddle in the Antartic, the baby penguins snuggle

U nder their dads' bellies

I ce is everywhere

N ever let a baby penguin sit on the ice!

Orlando Montgomery Dino Burns-Tucker (5)
Middleton Primary School, Middleton

What Am I?

I have a long, black tongue to help me
to get leaves off trees.
My skin has fur like brown potatoes.
I roam around in groups in a hot country.
I can grow to be five metres tall.
I am a herbivore.
Males are called bulls.
What am I?

Answer: A giraffe.

Dani Gallagher (7)
Middleton Primary School, Middleton

Munch, Munch!

P aws - big, furry, sharp claws

A nd I like to munch on bamboo

N ow there are only 1,000 of me left in the wild

D o you know I eat all day long?

A ll of my family live in the mountains of central China.

Chloe Long (6)
Middleton Primary School, Middleton

A Cheetah Sense Poem

He gets some meat and he starts running
He tastes the poor rabbit
He is the fastest animal on Earth
The Sahara Desert feels hot on his paws
He can hear galloping zebras
He can smell dust.

Anna Griffiths (6)

Middleton Primary School, Middleton

What Am I?

I smell delicious fish
My baby is called a cub
I have got a thick coat on my skin
to keep me warm
I have sharp claws and sharp white teeth
What am I?

Answer: A lion.

Beau Cecil James Burn-Tucker (5)
Middleton Primary School, Middleton

What Am I?

I am furry.
I am a carnivore.
I am yellow.
Our babies are called cubs.
I am the king of the jungle.
What am I?

Answer: A lion.

Percy Reynolds (6)
Middleton Primary School, Middleton

Winter

I can feel soft and freezing snow.
I can feel cold, aching hands.
I can smell hot gingerbread biscuits
in the oven.
I can smell my hot chocolate
and bundles of marshmallows.
I can see the cold winter and freezing trees.
I can see soft snow falling down.
I can hear cars crunching in the snow.
I can hear footsteps crunching on the ice.
I can taste warm, tasty
brown hot chocolate.
I can taste the roast dinner on my table.

Toby Luptak (6)
Norwich Primary Academy, Norwich

Winter

W oolly hats are good to wear

I cicles are really cold in winter

N apping in winter is very good

T he penguins waddle around in winter in the cold

E veryone needs to have a roast dinner

R umbling down the hills that are snowy, sparkly and shiny.

Beate Odrija Avina (7)

Norwich Primary Academy, Norwich

Winter

I can smell hot chocolate, gingerbread men
and a roast dinner.
I can see ice on the road and on the paths.
I can hear car sirens and cars
scraping their wheels.
I can feel freezing, crunchy snow.
I can taste cold, freezing snow
and hot chocolate.

Harry David Allen (6)
Norwich Primary Academy, Norwich

Winter

I can smell a nice, warm gingerbread man
in the oven.
I can hear people learning how to ice skate.
I can see cars covered in snow and I can
also see Christmas trees in the distance.
I can feel cold, aching hands.
I can taste warm, brown hot chocolate.

Tudor Ianis Negraru (6)
Norwich Primary Academy, Norwich

Winter

W oolly hats are good to wear

I cicles are sharp so be aware

N apping all winter long

T rees don't have leaves

E ating yummy, warm, healthy, cheerful, roast dinners

R olling down the snow, cold hills.

Phoebe Grady (6)

Norwich Primary Academy, Norwich

Winter

I can see cold snow in the trees.
I can smell a roast dinner
on the table in the lounge.
I can hear robins pecking on my bird food.
I can taste spaghetti hoops.
I can feel the cold, white snow on my hands.

Leia Batson (7)

Norwich Primary Academy, Norwich

Winter

I can see snowflakes
falling down from the sky.
I can taste the fresh air in my mouth.
I can smell the white snow.
I can hear sirens and birds
tweeting in their nests.
I can feel the icy trees.

Kyra Young (7)
Norwich Primary Academy, Norwich

Winter

I can see snowy white snowflakes.
I can hear fast cars
crunching on the white ice.
I can taste brown, warm hot chocolate.
I can smell hot gingerbread biscuits.
I can feel white, cold, aching snow.

Cyril Chigozie Akomah (6)
Norwich Primary Academy, Norwich

Winter

I can see cold winter trees in the darkness.
I can hear cars speeding into the distance.
I can smell lovely gingerbread men
in the oven.
I can feel cold, aching hands.
I can taste hot chocolate.

Rio Walker (6)
Norwich Primary Academy, Norwich

Winter

I can feel a soft, crunchy tree with branches.
I can hear crunchy snow on a car.
I can taste yummy hot chocolate.
I can see icy trees and snow falling down.
I can smell the coldness from the snow.

Kayden Rogers (6)

Norwich Primary Academy, Norwich

Winter

I can see a Christmas tree
glowing in the distance.
I can feel crunchy ice and snow.
I can hear cars crunching in the ice.
I can smell ginger cookies in the oven.
I can taste a roast dinner.

Zofia Misztal (6)
Norwich Primary Academy, Norwich

A Winter Poem

W arm as toast

I ndoors, by the fire, we roast

N umb fingers and toes

T he windows and doors are closed

E ight inches of snow

R ed, rosy cheeks glow.

Izzy Burrows (7)

Norwich Primary Academy, Norwich

Winter

I can see love from everyone at Christmas.
I can smell freshly-baked cinnamon.
I can hear twinkly games at Christmas.
I can taste yummy cookies at Christmas.
I can feel freezing cold snow.

Csenge Toth (6)
Norwich Primary Academy, Norwich

Winter

I can taste warm, brown hot chocolate.
I can see cold, soft, white snow.
I can smell my mum
cooking the roast dinner.
I can feel my cold, aching hands.
I can hear fireworks banging.

Riley Ayre (6)
Norwich Primary Academy, Norwich

Winter

I can smell cold, freezing snow.
I can hear cars crunching on the ice.
I can see soft snow falling down.
I can taste warm, tasty hot chocolate.
I can touch the freezing snow.

Lily-Louise Callaway (6)
Norwich Primary Academy, Norwich

Winter

I can see cold, white snow
I can feel snowflakes on my hand
I can hear footsteps in the ice
I can taste hot chocolate
I can smell chocolates on the tree.

Josie-Rose Christine Leader (7)
Norwich Primary Academy, Norwich

Hands

I can see the cold winter
I can feel cold aching hands
I can smell hot chocolate
I can hear cars
I can taste warm hot chocolate.

Cameron Marshall (7)
Norwich Primary Academy, Norwich

The Superhero

S uper Unicorn is flying in the air to stop the villain

U nicorn's friends help her to destroy the villain

P eople run from the evil unicorn

E vil Unicorn is destroyed by Super Unicorn, everyone cheers!

R obot Unicorn says, "Beep, boop!"

H eroes shout, "Hooray to Super Unicorn!"

E veryone cheers, "Hooray!"

R obot Unicorn is proud

O range sky, it is sunset now.

Jennyfer May Rippingale (6)
Suffield Park Infant School, Cromer

Superhero Superman

S uperhero excitedly flies like a superhero

U p and down, he flies through the sky like an eagle!

P eople need saving, "Please, help them!"

E very kid in the world is freezing

R elieved, the superhero has saved the day

H ere we go on our adventure, swooping like a bird

E verywhere is perfect, the day is saved

R unning as quickly as he can through town

O nly Superman can do this job!

Amelie Medler (6)
Suffield Park Infant School, Cromer

The Superhero

S uperheroes run fast when they're on a mission

U nderground, an adventure

P eople in the way

"E xcuse me," they couldn't hear me, the end of the road, jumping but it's a long way down

"R un, run fast, I don't want you to hurt yourself."

H ero saved the day as always

E veryone claps

R ules are rules to superheroes

O verall, it was a good day.

Jessica Folwer (6)

Suffield Park Infant School, Cromer

A Superhero

S uperheroes flying in the sky

U p in the air are superheroes

P eople are in trouble, they need help

E verything has been frozen by Jack Frost

R eading are the pink and purple superheroes, when their alarms go off, someone is in trouble and needs help

H eroes save people

E veryone is safe from the Joker

R elief! Everyone loves the superheroes

O h no, the Joker is here!

Mollie Taylor (7)
Suffield Park Infant School, Cromer

A Superhero

S uperhero swooping in the air like a hawk
U nder the clouds stand people in danger!
P eople fighting, people come to help
E verywhere, there are superheroes
"R eady superhero? Let's go!"
H ero to the rescue
E verything is frozen, superheroes come to help
R oyal superheroes in the mix
O range buildings, superheroes figure it out.

Raj Dorras (6)

Suffield Park Infant School, Cromer

The Superhero

S uperheroes running through the sky

U p in the air are superheroes

P eople need help everywhere they go

E veryone runs and cries

"R un! Run!" they cry again

"H urry, hurry!" cries the queen

E veryone is crying in fear!

"R un, run everyone!"

"O h, come back, the superhero has defeated it!"

Willow Elizabeth Davis (7)
Suffield Park Infant School, Cromer

The Superhero

S uperheroes shoot through the sky
U nderground, the superheroes search for the villain
P eople in danger, superheroes save them
E veryone is in danger
R unning mega fast
"H urry!" shouts the queen
E veryone shouts, "Superhero!"
"R each!" shouts someone
"O h no, a supervillain..."

Riley Stokes (6)

Suffield Park Infant School, Cromer

Superheroes

S uperhero is super
U nbelievable save, but how did it happen?
P eople are in danger, they need help
E xcellent save by the superhero
R un away, the villains are coming
"H urry, I need help!"
E asy for a superhero
R each up high to touch the superhero
O ver and under goes the superhero!

Noah Crane (6)
Suffield Park Infant School, Cromer

A Superhero

S uperheroes save the day

U nder the clouds there are superheroes

P eople are fighting crime

E verywhere, there are superheroes

"R eady superhero? Let's go!"

H ero is on his way

E veryone goes home

"R un, run everybody!"

O n the river, a superhero saves a person.

Luke Records (6)

Suffield Park Infant School, Cromer

The Superhero

S uperhero out saving people
U p in the sky, superheroes are flying
P eople saved by a superhero
E veryone will be saved
"R un away everyone!"
"H urry up, I need saving!"
E asy, this is easy for a superhero
R unning really fast
O ne superhero saved the day.

Sidney Jonas (7)
Suffield Park Infant School, Cromer

Superheroes

S uperheroes zooming in the sky
U p in the sky, they are flying
P eople enjoying the superheroes
E veryone is having fun
R unning very fast
H iding, "Come out, come out, wherever you are!"
E veryone loves a superhero
R unning everywhere
O ut of the air.

Isabella Waplington (6)

Suffield Park Infant School, Cromer

A Superhero

S uperhero saves the day
U p in the air are superheroes
P eople get saved
E verything is frozen
R eading books everywhere
H igh in the sky, there is a superhero
E veryone is cool like superheroes
R unning into the air
O n the river, a superhero saves the day.

Rokas Kriksciunas (6)
Suffield Park Infant School, Cromer

The Superhero

S uperheroes swoop down to save people
U p in the air, they are flying
P eople are trapped because of a fire
E veryone claps
R eaching the person
H anging from a cliff
E xcellent superpowers
R obots are scared of him
O ver the hill, there's the superhero.

Sebastian Edward-Ipperciel (7)

Suffield Park Infant School, Cromer

A Superhero

S uperheroes save the day
U p in the air are superheroes
P eople are in danger, let's save them!
E ach superhero is fun
R each up high, the superheroes are there
H ere they are!
E xcellent superheroes
R each up, there they are
O ver there, a superhero!

Bella Vanzino (7)
Suffield Park Infant School, Cromer

Superheroes

S uperman flying up high

U nicorn Girl is trotting to save the day

P eople are in trouble

E xcellent work heroes

R un away, a villain is trying to catch them!

H eroes saving the day

E veryone runs away

R obin saves the day

O n time!

Olga Fox (6)
Suffield Park Infant School, Cromer

A Superhero

S uperheroes can go fast

U p in the air, flying quickly

P eople run away

E verything is covered with ice

R un away from the baddies

H eroes can do their jobs

E verywhere is cold

R un from the Crusher

O ver the hill is a hero!

Ethan McVeigh (7)
Suffield Park Infant School, Cromer

Superheroes

S uperhero flies in the sky like an eagle
U p he goes
P eople think he's great
E verybody is scared
R unning fast
H ere he goes
E ach day, he helps people
R unning fast
O n the river, the superhero saves a person.

Chloe Findlay (6)
Suffield Park Infant School, Cromer

A Superhero

S pider-Man climbs walls

U p a wall he climbs

P eople think he is brave

E verybody cheers

R un fast

H ere comes a person

E ach day, a superhero comes

R unning fast

O n time.

Migle Mickeviciute (7)
Suffield Park Infant School, Cromer

Superhero

My superhero is as strong as a cheetah
My superhero is speedy like a lion
My superhero is as brave as a panther
My superhero is clever
My superhero is powerful like a tiger
My superhero is helpful like a mum.

Jacob Grant (7)
Suffield Park Infant School, Cromer

Heroes

H elpful
E verybody
R emember them
O nly help people in need
E veryone loves them
S trong.

Andre Bandarra (6)
Suffield Park Infant School, Cromer

Heroes

H eroes

E xcellent

R ushing to save the day

O ne in a million

E xcited

S uper.

Darcie Goodwin (7)
Suffield Park Infant School, Cromer

Heroes

H elping people
E xcellent
R ight things they do
O n the go
E veryone
S uper!

Patryk Imienionek (6)

Suffield Park Infant School, Cromer

Heroes

H elpful

E veryone

R escued

O n the run

E xcellent

S uper!

Hayley Jena Chatten (7)

Suffield Park Infant School, Cromer

Heroes

H elping
E veryone
R umbling
O xygen
E xcellent
S uper.

Emelia McVeigh (7)
Suffield Park Infant School, Cromer

Heroes

H appy
E xcellent
R escuing
O n the go
E xcited
S uper

William Smith (7)

Suffield Park Infant School, Cromer

Hero On The Go

H elpful

E xcellent

R escuing everybody

O n the go.

Elicia Garcia (6)
Suffield Park Infant School, Cromer

A Hero

H elpful

E xcited

R escuing

O ne way to go...

Chelsea Gao (6)

Suffield Park Infant School, Cromer

A Hero

H appy
E xcellent
R ight
O n the go.

Evie Plummer (6)
Suffield Park Infant School, Cromer

Heroes

H eroes

E verybody is

R eady

G **O** !

Cody Pegg (6)

Suffield Park Infant School, Cromer

Young Writers Information

We hope you have enjoyed reading this book – and that you will continue to in the coming years.

If you're a young writer who enjoys reading and creative writing, or the parent of an enthusiastic poet or story writer, do visit our website **www.youngwriters.co.uk**. Here you will find free competitions, workshops and games, as well as recommended reads, a poetry glossary and our blog.

If you would like to order further copies of this book, or any of our other titles, then please give us a call or visit **www.youngwriters.co.uk**.

Young Writers
Remus House
Coltsfoot Drive
Peterborough
PE2 9BF
(01733) 890066
info@youngwriters.co.uk

 @YoungWritersUK @YoungWritersCW